WITHDRAWN

The Biography of Corn

L. Michelle Nielsen

Crabtree Publishing Company
www.crabtreebooks.com

Crabtree Publishing Company
www.crabtreebooks.com

To my best friend Andrea, who always appreciates a corny sentiment.

Coordinating editor: Ellen Rodger
Series editor: Carrie Gleason
Project editor: Adrianna Morganelli
Design and production coordinator: Rosie Gowsell
Production assistance and layout: Samara Parent
Art direction: Rob MacGregor
Photo research: Allison Napier
Prepress technician: Nancy Johnson

Photo Credits: Chad Ehlers/Alamy: p. 5 (top); David R. Frazier Photolibrary, Inc./Alamy: p. 26 (bottom); tbkmedia.de/Alamy: p. 7; Jim West/Alamy: p. 21 (top); AP Photo/ Pieter Malan: p. 31; AP Photo/Moises Castillo: p. 30 (top); AP Photo/Scanpix, Erik Johansen: p. 25 (bottom); AP Photo/West Central Tribune, Bill Zimmer: p. 28; AP Photo/Obed Zilwa: p. 30 (bottom); Biblioteca Medicea-Laurenziana, Florence, Italy/The Bridgeman Art Library: p. 10 (bottom); British Museum, London, UK/The Bridgeman Art Library: p. 12; Museum of Fine Arts, Houston, Texas, USA, Museum purchase funded by 'One Great Night in November 1990/The Bridgeman Art Library: p. 5 (bottom); Private Collection, Peter Newark American Pictures/The Bridgeman Art Library: p. 14 (bottom); Private Collection, Photo © Boltin Picture Library/The Bridgeman Art Library: p. 11 (top); Private Collection, Photo © Bonhams, London, UK/The Bridgeman Art Library: p. 13 (bottom); Private Collection, The Stapleton Collection/The Bridgeman Art Library: p. 11 (bottom); Service Historique de la Marine, Vincennes, France, Giraudon/The Bridgeman Art Library: p. 15 (top); Peter Beck/Corbis: p. 22; Bettmann/Corbis: p. 23 (top); Mike Boyatt/Corbis: p. 18 (middle); Corbis: p. 8 (top), p. 18 (top), p. 20; Matthias Kulka/zefa/Corbis: p. 25 (top); Gideon Mendel/Corbis: p. 1; Lake County Museum/Corbis: p. 6 (top); Scott Sinklier/Corbis: cover; Liba Taylor/Corbis: p. 17 (bottom); The Granger Collection, New York: p. 14 (top), p. 16, p. 17 (top); Diccon Alexander/Photo Researchers, Inc.: p. 13 (top); Scott Camazine/Photo Researchers, Inc. p. 29 (top); David R. Frazier/Photo Researchers, Inc.: p. 19 (top); Joyce Photographics/Photo Researchers, Inc.: p. 9 (bottom left); Astrid & Hanns-Frieder Michler/Photo Researchers, Inc.: p. 29 (bottom); Steve Percival/Photo Researchers, Inc.: p. 21 (bottom); Phanie/Photo Researchers, Inc.: p. 8 (bottom), p. 24; Gregory K. Scott/Photo Researchers, Inc.: p. 9 (top). Other images from stock CD

Cartography: Jim Chernishenko: p. 6

Cover: A farmer in Iowa, in the United States, harvests corn.

Title page: A woman in Zimbabwe, Africa, picks corn in a cornfield.

Contents page: Popcorn was first cultivated by Mesoamericans and is a popular treat today.

Library and Archives Canada Cataloguing in Publication

Nielsen, L. Michelle
    The Biography of Corn / L. Michelle Nielson.

(How did that get here?)
Includes index.
ISBN 978-0-7787-2491-9 (bound)
ISBN 978-0-7787-2527-5 (pbk.)

    1. Corn--Juvenile literature. I. Title. II. Series.

SB191.M2N53 2007   j633.1'5   C2007-900699-X

Library of Congress Cataloging-in-Publication Data

Nielsen, L. Michelle.
    The Biography of Corn / written by L. Michelle Nielsen.
      p. cm. -- (How did that get here?)
    Includes index.
    ISBN-13: 978-0-7787-2491-9 (rlb.)
    ISBN-10: 0-7787-2491-3 (rlb.)
    ISBN-13: 978-0-7787-2527-5 (pb.)
    ISBN-10: 0-7787-2527-8 (pb.)
    1. Corn--Juvenile literature. I. Title. II. Series.

SB191.M2N54 2007
633.1'5--dc22
                           2007003457

Crabtree Publishing Company

www.crabtreebooks.com   1-800-387-7650

Published in Canada
Crabtree Publishing
616 Welland Ave.
St. Catharines, ON
L2M 5V6

Published in the United States
Crabtree Publishing
PMB16A
350 Fifth Ave., Suite 3308
New York, NY 10118

Published in the United Kingdom
Crabtree Publishing
White Cross Mills
High Town, Lancaster
LA1 4XS

Published in Australia
Crabtree Publishing
386 Mt. Alexander Rd.
Ascot Vale (Melbourne)
VIC 3032

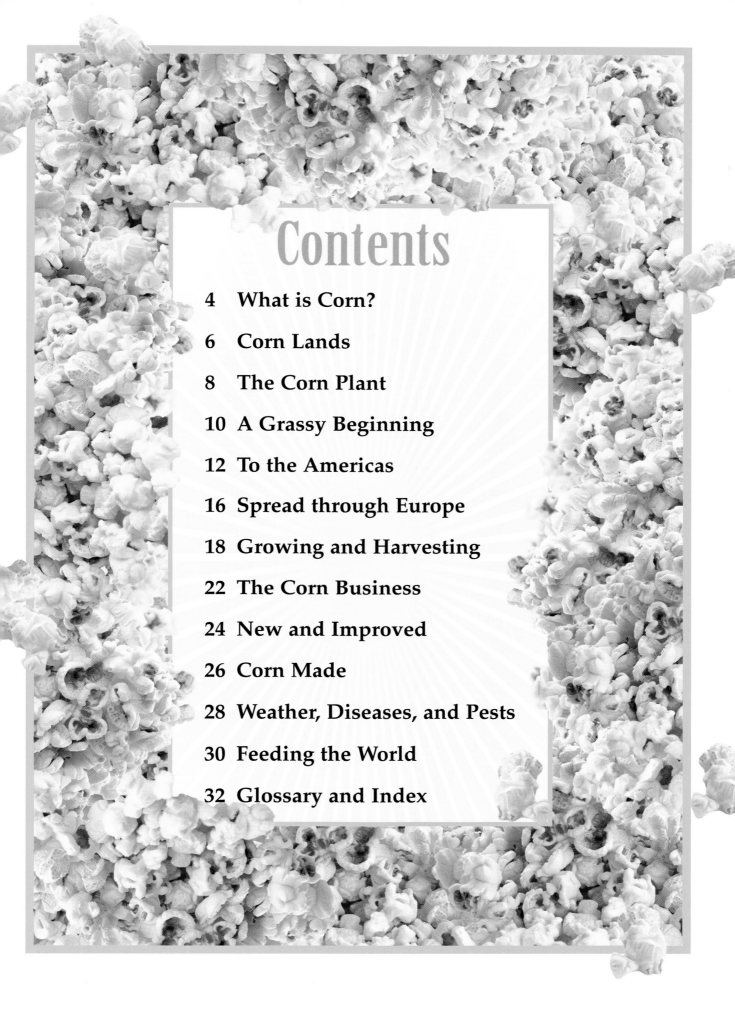

Contents

What is Corn?

Corn is a cereal, or a type of grass that produces a grain people and animals eat. There are thousands of different varieties of corn that are grown almost everywhere in the world, each one able to grow in different environments, from deserts, to flat plains, and mountainsides. Corn is an important source of food, especially for people in **developing countries**, and it is an ingredient in many products, including soft drinks, ice cream, paint, paper, and rubber. The many uses of corn make it a valuable commodity. A commodity is a product that is bought and sold by individuals and businesses all over the world.

First Cultivators

Corn was first **cultivated** as early as 5000 B.C, by Mesoamericans, the ancient peoples of Mexico and Central America. Corn spread to the Caribbean islands, and North and South America. When Christopher Columbus, an explorer who sailed for Spain, arrived in the **New World**, in 1492, his crew came across corn in Cuba. The island's native peoples, the Taino, called corn *mahiz*, meaning "source of life." They used corn to make food, such as cakes made of ground corn. Realizing corn's value as a food source, the Spanish brought it back to Europe, calling it *maíz,* which was translated in English as "maize."

▶ *The scientific name for corn is* **Zea mays***. It is a cereal grass, a family of plants that also includes wheat, oats, and rice.*

From Food to Fuel

Many people in North America eat corn on the cob, and heat corn kernels to make popcorn, but most corn is used to make thousands of different products. The majority of corn grown in the United States is made into feed for livestock, such as cattle and poultry. Soft drinks are often sweetened using a sweetener made from corn, and many food products are made with corn as well, such as corn flour, corn syrup, and corn oil. Some cars and other machines are even powered by a liquid fuel called ethanol, which is made from corn.

(right) Corn helps save people in developing countries from starving. Many farmers, especially in Africa, grow corn to feed their families. These women are grinding corn to make mealie meal, or corn meal.

Corn Gods

Many ancient peoples native to North, South, and Central America believed in many gods, including corn gods. Ceremonies that included prayer, singing, and dancing were held at different stages of corn production, such as planting, plowing, and harvesting. The people believed if they made the corn gods happy, they would ensure that enough corn was produced to feed all the people in the community. Some peoples, including the Maya and Aztec of Mesoamerica, believed that the best way to honor the gods was to offer them gifts of blood. Some Mayan farmers inflicted wounds on themselves and spread the blood over the soil in an effort to please the gods and ensure a good harvest of corn.

▼ *Mesoamericans used grinding stones, such as this one, to grind corn during ceremonies.*

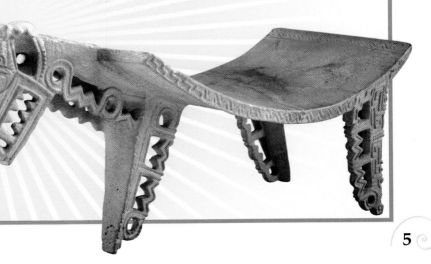

Corn Lands

When Europeans first came to the Americas in the late 1400s, corn had spread from its origins in Mexico and Central America to the southern regions of present-day Canada and as far south as Chile in South America. Once taken back to Europe, corn seeds were quickly traded all over Europe, Asia, and Africa. Today, almost 85 percent of the countries in the world grow corn. Unlike other plants, corn has adapted, or changed, to suit the many environments it is grown in. There are different types of corn that can grow in dry or wet soils, in areas with cool temperatures or in **tropical** zones, and in valleys, on plains, hills, and mountainsides.

© CURT TEICH & CO., INC.

▲ *The Corn Belt in the United States has ideal conditions for producing many types of corn and is the source of 80 percent of American corn.*

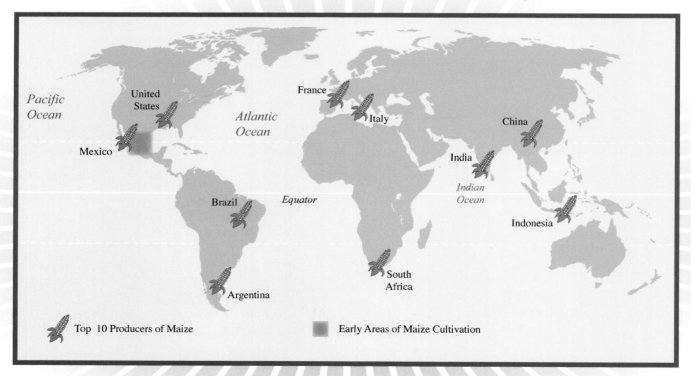

Top 10 Producers of Maize   Early Areas of Maize Cultivation

This map shows where most of the world's corn is grown today, as well as where it originated. It is grown all over the world, and does especially well in temperate zones, or areas with mild climates.

Corn Leaders

The United States is the world's top corn producer, cultivating over 308 million tons (280 million tonnes) a year. Over 40 percent of all corn produced worldwide is grown in the United States. While most of that corn is used in the United States to feed livestock and make products, 20 percent is exported, or sold to other countries. China and Brazil are also major producers of corn. China, as the second largest producer, still grows less than half of that grown by the United States. Not all countries produce the amount of corn they need, and must import, or buy in, the cereal grain from other countries. Japan is the top importer of corn in the world, buying most of its corn from the United States. Other countries that import a lot of corn every year are Mexico, Canada, Taiwan, and Egypt.

The Corn Belt

The Corn Belt is the area in the middle of the United States where more than 80 percent of American corn is produced. The Corn Belt covers parts of Ohio, Illinois, Indiana, Missouri, Kansas, Iowa, Michigan, Minnesota, Missouri, and Nebraska. These areas have fertile, or nutrient-rich, soil and temperate conditions, which means it is never too hot or too cold. These are the best conditions for growing many types of corn, allowing farmers to produce healthy crops each year. The favorable growing conditions of the Corn Belt have made the United States the top producer of corn in the world.

(above) Ears of dry corn hang in China, one of the top corn-producing countries in the world.

The Corn Plant

A healthy corn plant consists of a thick, sturdy stem, a root system to collect water and nutrients from the soil, flowering parts, and leaves. Most corn plants have one or two cylinder-shaped ears that grow about half way down the stem. Ears are made up of rows of kernels and the cob, or the solid mass in the center that the kernels grow on. Ears are surrounded by coverings of leaves, called husks, that protect the kernels from insects, and fungi, which cause disease.

A World of Variety

Different varieties of corn plants look different from one another. A corn stalk can be as short as two feet (0.6 meters) in height or more than 20 feet (six meters) tall. Some corn plants produce ears, or corn cobs, that are a few inches long, and others have ears measuring up to two feet (0.6 meters) in length. Corn kernels come in a number of colors, including yellow, blue, white, red, or a mixture of two or more colors. There are thousands of varieties of corn, and each variety is categorized into groups that have similar characteristics.

◂ *Corn kernels are attached to the cob.*

(below) There are thousands of varieties of corn.

An "A-maize-ing" Plant

Like most plants, corn has male and female parts that work together to grow new plants. The male part of the plant is called the tassel. The tassel is located at the top of the corn stalk and is made up of spikelets, or tiny flowers that produce **pollen**. The corn plant also has female parts, which is the ear of kernels, or seeds. Each seed has a long, thread-like silk growing out of it. Since each cob usually has between 500 and 1,200 kernels, hundreds of silks emerge from the top of the ear, which is encased by the husk. The tassel releases millions of grains of pollen into the air, which is carried by the wind. The pollen sticks to the silks and pollinates the seeds. Pollination creates seeds that can be planted to grow new corn stalks. The seeds increase in size until the ear is ready to be harvested, or picked.

(above) The male part of the corn plant is called the tassle.

Seed of Life

A kernel, or seed, contains all the parts to grow into a new corn plant. Inside the seed is an embryo, which is the part that develops into a new plant. There is also a starchy, or energy-rich, section called the endosperm. The endosperm is the food the embryo uses to grow into a healthy seedling, or young plant. The seed is surrounded by a hard seed coat, or covering, that protects the embryo and endosperm from getting crushed or damaged.

(above) The silks of sweet corn start out green and turn brown when the ear is ready to be harvested or picked.

Helping Out Mother Nature

The seeds of most plants in the wild are spread by the wind, and in the dung of birds and animals that eat the seeds and then expel them in new places. Corn seeds are not spread in these ways because they are protected by husks. The only way for a new corn plant to grow is if each individual seed is planted. If people stopped planting corn seeds, corn would become extinct, or disappear from the planet.

A Grassy Beginning

The first corn plants grew in Mesoamerica, or present-day southern Mexico and Central America. These early plants had small ears and far fewer kernels than today's corn plants. Scientists do not agree about how the original corn plant evolved, or changed, into a plant similar to the corn plants grown today. Many scientists believe that different grass plants crossed, or mated to create corn plants. As early as 5000 B.C., groups of people in Mesoamerica, began cultivating corn, or growing it as a crop. Corn soon became a staple of their diet. A staple food is the main part of a diet and supplies most, but not all, of the nutrients people need.

(below) The Olmec are one of the oldest Mesoamerican civilizations. They were one of the first peoples to set up farming villages, where they grew corn.

Selection

Mesoamerican farmers used a process called selection, or selective **breeding**, to create varieties of corn that had beneficial, or useful, characteristics. Selection involved choosing the healthiest corn plants from a crop and using the seeds to plant a new crop. For example, if an ear of corn had more kernels than normal, its seeds were planted the next year, which would result in more plants that produced ears with many kernels. Selection was also used when corn was taken to new areas to be grown. When seeds were planted in a new area with a different environment, such as an area with less rainfall, some of the plants did poorly while others thrived. The corn plant continued to adapt, or change, over thousands of years, leading to new varieties of corn suited to new environments. Mesoamericans developed hundreds of new varieties of corn this way.

(above) Popcorn is the oldest type of corn cultivated by early Mesoamericans. It spread across North and South America and was used by different Native groups for food and to make jewelry and decorations.

The Maya

The Maya was a Mesoamerican civilization that existed between 250 A.D. and 950 A.D. in southern Mexico. The Maya used corn as a staple food crop. They honored corn gods to ensure healthy crops each year through ceremonies, human sacrifices, and prayer. The Maya relied on farming, especially corn, to feed the people who lived in the villages and cities throughout their lands. Like other Mesoamerican peoples before them, the Maya ate corn off the cob, roasted and boiled it, and used stone plates, called *metates*, to grind the kernels. The ground corn was added to drinks and made into a thin bread called a tortilla, which is still a popular food in Mexico today.

The Aztec

The Aztec lived in Central Mexico from 1200 to 1521. The Aztec conquered, or took over, the lands of many neighboring Mesoamerican peoples, expanding their empire. They collected **taxes** from the people, which could be paid in many forms, including with corn. The Aztec capital city of Tenochtitlan was built on an island in Lake Texcoco, which is present-day Mexico City. Surrounding the city were *chinampas*, or floating gardens, where corn and other crops were grown. Frames made of reeds were anchored to the bottom of the lake, and a layer of soil deep enough to plant the crops was put on top of the frames.

▲ *One of the Maya corn gods was* **Yum Kaaz.** *He was shown in sculptures and other art forms as a young man with silky long hair and a headdress made of corn stalks and leaves.*

◄ *The Maya and Aztec used all parts of the corn plant. Corn was ground into grain to make tortillas. The husks were used to wrap up tamales, a traditional food of meat wrapped in corn dough. Corn stalks were often dried and used as fence posts.*

11

To the Americas

Corn did not stay within Mesoamerica. Mostly through trade between peoples, it spread to islands in the Caribbean, South America as far south as present-day Chile, and as far north as the southern regions of present-day Canada. Different varieties of corn were produced to suit the many environments the plant was taken to. Each ear of corn produced hundreds of kernels, so when corn was brought to a community, it provided the people with a lot of food. Some nomadic peoples, or people that moved around hunting and gathering food, formed permanent farming settlements because corn provided them with a food staple.

To South America

As early as 3000 B.C., traders brought corn seeds from Mesoamerica to South America. At first, corn was mainly cultivated along the west coast in the Andes Mountains. Corn, potatoes, tomatoes, and other crops were grown on the mountains on terraces. Terraces looked like steps cut into the sides of a mountain. Fertile soil was brought to each step to even out the ground, and crops were planted. By 1500 B.C., corn had also spread to eastern South America.

Most of the Native peoples in North, South, and Central America believed that nature, including corn crops, was linked to gods. They tried to please the gods by honoring them in ceremonies. Native peoples believed that happy gods would make sure enough food grew for everyone in the community.

The Inca's Real Gold

The Inca were a powerful people who lived in South America between 1200 and the mid-1500s. At its most powerful, the Inca **empire** extended from present-day Colombia in the north to Chile in the south, ruling over six million people. The Inca empire grew by conquering surrounding Native groups and taking their lands. While the Inca were proud of their art forms, including sculptures and masks made of gold, they were an agricultural, or farming, peoples, who valued crops. Corn and potatoes were the most important foods in Inca society. When a new land was conquered, one of the first things the Inca did was to prepare the soil for corn crops. Large amounts of corn were needed to feed all the people who lived in the empire. Corn was also burned during ceremonies to honor the gods, and to make *chicha*, a type of beer drunk mostly by Inca rulers and nobles after battle victories and during ceremonies. *Chicha* is still made by the **descendants** of Inca peoples today.

(above) The Inca used terrace farming to grow their crops. Corn grew on the lower terraces where it was warmer, while potatoes grew higher up where it was cooler.

(above) The Inca's main god was the Sun god. People believed the Sapa Inca, or Inca emperor, was a descendant of the Sun god.

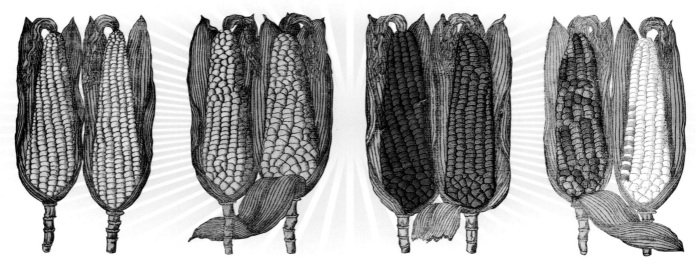

To North America

Around 1200 B.C., corn was grown in present-day New Mexico and Arizona. It was difficult to grow crops there because of the dry, sandy soil. The Native peoples living in the area, such as the Hopi and the Zuni, developed ways of farming to help the plants grow. Seeds were planted deep in the ground, where the soil was moist. Canals and other types of **irrigation systems** were built to bring what little rainwater fell to the crops. Corn quickly became a staple in the diets of the Native peoples of the Southwest. They added corn to stews, popped popcorn, and made breads with ground corn.

(top) Native groups often grew many different types of corn, and cross-pollinated *them to make new varieties. Many types of corn contained kernels of various colors, including yellow, red, purple, blue, and white.*

(right) This picture from 1902 shows a Hopi man farming corn that adapted to the dry conditions of the American southwest.

Eastwards and Upwards

Farming was practiced mostly by Native peoples who lived in the southwest and east of the present-day United States. Corn reached the eastern part of North America around 200 A.D. Squash and beans were already being grown by many Native groups in the east. Corn was first grown in small amounts but eventually became a staple crop of many Native groups from present-day Florida to southern Canada. In most Native groups, it was the women's job to grow and harvest the corn, while the men fished and hunted animals for meat. The women used a stick to make a hole in the soil, and dropped four to six seed kernels in each hole. Native peoples throughout North America sang to spirits while they planted corn, hoping they would grant them a healthy crop.

Native farmers grew enough corn to feed the people. Leftover corn was stored in case the next year's harvest was poor.

The Three Sisters

▼ The "Three Sisters": corn, squash, and beans.

On its own, corn does not provide all of the nutrients and vitamins people need to stay healthy. Native peoples combined corn with other vegetables, often beans and squash. The trio of plants became known as the "Three Sisters" among the Iroquois nation of the Great Lakes region. The "Three Sisters" also helped each other grow. Corn was planted first, and after growing for a few weeks, the beans and squash were planted along side the corn stalk. The beans provided nitrogen for the soil, which acted as a fertilizer and helped the corn and squash grow. The corn stalk provided a support for the bean plant, which wound around the stalk, growing up toward the sunlight. The squash plants grew low to the ground. Their leaves provided a ground cover that helped prevent weeds from growing and sucking nutrients from the soil that were needed by all three plants.

Spread through Europe

European explorers began arriving in the New World in the late 1400s. They were on journeys of discovery, looking to claim new lands and valuable goods to take back to their home countries. Many of the goods these explorers brought back were crops that were native to the New World, including potatoes, **cacao beans**, vanilla beans, and corn.

(above) Before 1492, Europeans did not know the continents of North and South America existed. Early explorers who landed in the New World had originally set sail in search of a sea route to Asia. When Columbus brought back riches, including plants, from the New World he was honored by the King and Queen of Spain.

Feeding Europe

In 1492, Christopher Columbus landed on the present-day island of Cuba in the **West Indies**. His crew watched the inhabitants of the island, the Taino, grind corn kernels into a flour to make cakes and other foods. European explorers realized corn was a valuable source of food. When Columbus brought the kernels back to Europe, they were immediately planted in Spain, and quickly spread across southern Europe. Corn became popular, especially with the poor, because it was less expensive than wheat, the main grain grown throughout most of Europe. Corn also created more food. By the end of the 1500s, corn had spread to most countries in Europe.

To the Far East

Explorers from countries all over Europe followed in Columbus' footsteps, journeying to the New World, and bringing back valuable goods. Explorers who traveled to South America brought back types of corn that were different than those Columbus had found. By the mid-1500s, Portuguese merchant, or trading, ships brought corn to China and India, and used it to trade for valuable items only found in those countries, including spices and silk.

Corn Aboard

The Portuguese began traveling to Africa in the 1440s to trade goods for African slaves. By the 1500s, there was a growing demand for slaves in New World **colonies** to work on settlers' **plantations** and in mines. The Portuguese and other European merchants set up trading posts along the west coast of Africa, where they introduced corn to African farmers. Corn provided more food than sorghum and millet, two cereal grains that were grown throughout much of Africa, and spread throughout the continent. Portuguese slave traders purchased corn grown by African farmers to feed slaves on their journeys across the Atlantic. Corn became a profitable business for African farmers around slave ports on the west coast of Africa.

(above) Each slave aboard a ship received about two pounds (0.9 kilograms) of corn a day during the Atlantic crossing.

▸ *Today, corn is a staple crop throughout Africa, especially in Kenya, Uganda, and South Africa.*

17

Growing and Harvesting

Today, the techniques used to farm different varieties of corn are similar. On large farms, machines called corn planters are used to plant corn in rows about 30 inches (76 centimeters) apart. Corn planters make furrows in the soil about three to four inches (eight to ten centimeters) deep, and disperse seeds inside them. Planters are pulled by tractors and can plant eight to 16 rows at one time. The cornfield's soil must be warmer than 50° Fahrenheit (10° Celsius) for seeds to germinate, or sprout new plants. It can take from two days to several weeks before a corn seedling pops up above the soil.

Growing Healthy Plants

Corn plants need specific nutrients to grow. Phosphorus and nitrogen are nutrients often added to the soil in chemical fertilizers or animal manure. Without them, corn plants take longer to grow, are unhealthy, and produce fewer kernels. Farmers also ensure nutrient-rich soil by rotating their crops. In crop rotation, one type of crop is grown in a field one season, and a different crop in the same field the next season. Many farmers in the Corn Belt grow corn one season, and soybeans the next. Soybeans provide nitrogen for the soil. The nitrogen helps next year's corn plants grow into a healthy crop.

▲ *No-till planting means leaving the stalks in the fields after harvest and not plowing or tilling them under. The remaining plants act as a natural fertilizer.*

(top) A cornfield usually has 16,000 to 32,000 corn stalks per acre (0.4 hectare).

Harvesting

Today, corn is usually harvested by a machine called a combine, which is also used to harvest other cereal crops, such as wheat. A special attachment, called a corn head, is put on the front of the combine. The corn head is wide enough to cut down between six and eight rows in a cornfield at one time. It cuts the corn stalk just above the ground. The stalks are fed into the combine, where the ears are separated from the stalks, and the kernels are separated from the ears. The kernels are then stored in a tank in the combine, while all the leftover parts of the plant, including the stalks and leaves, are dumped back onto the field.

▶ *After a harvest, corn stalks and other parts of the plant are either left in the field to provide nutrients for the soil, or are collected to be used as feed for cattle and sheep.*

Combines are machines that combine the steps necessary to harvest corn. These steps include cutting down plants, and separating the ears and kernels from the stalks.

Drying and Storage

Kernels that will be stored for long periods of time must be dried to prevent them from spoiling, or rotting. Corn is dried by passing air over the kernels. Low temperature drying uses only a fan and outside air to dry the kernels, while high temperature drying uses fans that blow heated air onto the kernels. Care must be taken when using high temperature dryers because the kernels could crack, which lowers their quality and brings in less money for the farmer. The dried kernels must be kept at temperatures as low as 30° Fahrenheit (-1° Celsius) after they are dried to prevent mold from growing. Corn is stored in large bins called silos on a farm. Farmers can also take their corn to grain elevators, which are large buildings that store corn. Companies or people that own elevators buy corn from many farmers. They clean it, store it, and then sell it to refineries and food processors, or sell it to other countries.

Elevators store grains, such as wheat and corn.

Refining and Milling

A lot of the corn produced in the United States is sent to refineries and mills to be processed. Corn refineries are factories that separate corn kernels into their parts, using a process called wet milling. In wet milling, kernels are softened by soaking them in warm water. They are then cooked, ground by machines, and sent through screens and other devices to separate them into their parts, including the germ, or embryo, the endosperm, and seed coat. These parts are used to make food and **industrial** products. In dry milling, corn kernels are ground into a coarse grain called meal, a fine powdery substance called corn flour, or grains of other **consistencies**. The grain is sold to companies that make breakfast cereal, bread, and other products.

▸ *Ethanol is a fuel made from corn. Ethanol is sometimes added to gasoline to create a cleaner burning fuel.*

Corn refineries began making ethanol in the 1940s, but only in small amounts. Ethanol production picked up in the 1970s when gasoline, which is made from oil, was scarce.

The Corn Business

In the United States, Canada, and Europe, producing corn is a business. In developing countries corn is grown mainly as a subsistence crop, or a crop that feeds the farmers, their families, and their communities. Most corn in the United States is grown on large **commercial** farms. To make money, it is important for farms to produce high yields. A yield is the amount of healthy corn that is grown.

▾ *Tractors and other machines allow farmers to plant more corn than using hand tools and horse-pulled plows. More corn plants result in higher yields, earning farmers more money.*

An Industry of Corn

The American corn industry includes the individuals and businesses that contribute to the growth of corn, as well as the companies that make corn into products. The seed corn industry is also a major business. Seed corn are the kernels that are planted to grow new plants. Seed corn companies are often involved in researching and creating hybrid corn. Hybrid corn is produced from two different types of corn plants that are suited to specific environmental conditions, such as areas prone to drought. Seed corn companies grow crops that are harvested and sold only for planting new seeds. Farmers that grow hybrid plants cannot use the kernels from that crop to plant the following season. They must buy new seed each year, making seed corn a profitable business.

The Commodity Market

Commodities are goods that are bought and sold. The price of corn, like all commodities, goes up and down. Commodities that are in demand tend to have higher prices. In recent years, many more products have been using corn as an ingredient, such as corn-based plastics, and ethanol, which is a more environmentally-friendly fuel source. Prices of commodities also tend to increase if the supply, or yield, of a product is lower than normal. For example, if corn yields are lower than expected one year, due to storms or pest infestations, the price of the remaining corn will increase.

(above) Many well-known food products are made using corn. The Kellogg Company was established in 1906 by American Will Keith Kellogg. The company makes many breakfast cereals using corn, including Kellogg's Corn Flakes and Corn Pops.

Popcorn

Popcorn is the oldest type of corn, first cultivated by Mesoamericans and spread across North and South America. Each kernel has a very hard shell, and a small amount of water inside. When heated, the water turns into steam and pressure builds, causing the kernel to pop, expelling its white starchy interior. Popcorn became popular in the late 1800s when the first popcorn popper was invented to pop the kernels. This produced a lot of popcorn at once, and popcorn began to be sold at fairs, carnivals, and by vendors on the street. Popcorn increased in popularity during the **Great Depression**, because it was an inexpensive treat that people could afford.

New and Improved

Scientists and seed companies are now making new and improved varieties of corn plants. To increase corn yields, many farmers plant hybrid corn plants. A hybrid plant is made by cross-pollinating, or using the pollen of one variety of corn to fertilize a different type of corn. The seed that is produced then grows into a plant that has the characteristics, or features, of both parent plants. Hybrid plants are bred to suit specific environments. For example, one type of corn plant might produce many kernels but may also be vulnerable to insect infestation. Breeders can cross-pollinate the corn plant with a type of corn that the insects do not like to eat. The hybrid plant would then produce a lot of kernels and be resistant to the insects. This would result in healthier corn plants, and higher yields.

Designer Genes

Genes are substances that exist inside every **cell** of a corn plant, and determine what characteristics a plant has. A plant can have a gene that makes it more resistant to disease or require less water than other plants. Scientists have discovered what many different genes in corn plants do, and have created new types of corn, called genetically modified organisms, or GMOs, by modifying the genes of existing corn plants. This allows scientists to make corn plants that are resistant to disease, insects, and **drought**. Farmers that plant GMO plants do not have to buy pesticides and **fungicides**. Scientists have also made corn varieties that are more nutritious for people to eat.

GMO plants help the environment by reducing the amount of chemical pesticides and fungicides used. These chemicals pollute drinking water and the soil.

Biodiversity

Hybrid and GMO corn are important for producing high yields. In order to maintain biodiversity, or the variety of plants grown in the world, it is also important to grow and produce seeds for all types of corn, including the types that are hundreds of years old. New varieties of hybrid or GMO plants are often only successful for a limited amount of time because the environment the corn is planted in also changes. Insects and diseases often adapt, or change, and are eventually able to harm crops that were once resistant to them. Climates, or weather, in many areas around the world are also changing, and current types of corn may not grow well in these new conditions. By keeping as many varieties of corn alive as possible, it is more likely that at least one type of corn will exist or be created to withstand new diseases, pests, or weather conditions.

Many people do not think GMO plants should be made because no one knows for sure if they will cause future health problems for people and animals.

(left) Seedbanks are places that store hundreds of varieties of seeds, especially endangered types. One seedbank, on Spitzbergen island, in the Arctic Ocean, is located 1,312 feet (400 meters) below the ground and stores the seeds of many types of plants, including corn. These men are at a ceremony marking the opening of the bank in 2006.

Corn Made

Corn kernels are ground at refineries and made into products that are found in many kitchens, including corn oils, syrups, and starches. Corn oil comes from the germ of a corn kernel. Corn oil is used as an ingredient in many foods, including salad dressings and margarine. When cooking meals, many people use corn oil to add flavor and to prevent food from sticking to the pan. Corn oils are also found in paints and soaps.

Cornstarch and Corn Syrup

Cornstarch comes from the endosperm, or starchy part, of the corn kernel. It is a white powder that is used by food manufacturers to thicken desserts, including pie fillings, puddings, and yogurts. It is also an ingredient in crayons, batteries, paper, and disposable diapers, since some types of cornstarch can absorb up to 2,000 times their own weight in moisture. Corn syrup is a product of cornstarch, water, and other ingredients, often used in foods such as frostings, chocolate, peanut butter, and jellies to give them a smoother texture and sweeter taste.

▲ *Corn oil is made from the germs of kernels.*

(right) A factory that manufactures corn tortillas.

Corn Flour and Meal

Corn meal has been a staple in the diets of many people for thousands of years, especially those living in Mexico. Corn meal has a coarse texture and is made from ground kernels. It is used to make many traditional Mexican foods, such as tortillas, taco shells, and corn chips. Corn flour is made of kernels ground up to a finer powder than cornmeal, and is used in baked goods, and to thicken sauces and gravies.

▸ *Corn chips are made from corn meal.*

Ethanol

Ethanol is an alcohol made from many different plants, including corn. It is made at refineries by mixing corn or corn crop waste, such as stalks, with water and yeast, and heating the mixture. Ethanol can fuel tractors, cars, and other vehicles. It is a cleaner fuel than gasoline, releasing fewer **greenhouse gases** and other pollutants into the air. Ethanol has been used as a fuel for automobiles since the early 1900s. Today, few cars run on only ethanol, but ethanol is added to gasoline to create a cleaner burning fuel. Ethanol has become a large industry in the United States and Canada and has given farmers more customers to sell their crops to, such as refineries.

▸ *Many people enjoy sweet corn on the cob.*

▾ *In 1908, Henry Ford built a car called the Model T that could run on gasoline or ethanol.*

Sweet Corn

Sweet corn is the only type of corn eaten by people directly off the cob. In North America, corn on the cob is often an end of summer treat. It is best to eat sweet corn when it has just been harvested because that is when it is freshest and sweetest. People boil sweet corn on the cob, and flavor it with butter and salt. Sweet corn is also sold to food manufacturers. The kernels are removed from the cob and packaged as canned corn or frozen corn, both popular foods that can be bought at grocery stores all year long.

Feeding Animals

More than 60 percent of American corn is used to feed livestock, including cattle, sheep, poultry, and pigs. Most animal feed and pet foods are made from field corn, also called dent corn. When kernels are sent to corn refineries, some of the products made, such as corn **gluten** meal, which is high in **protein**, are used in animal feeds. These types of feeds are very nutritious and give animals energy. Silage is a type of feed made from cut up corn stalks. The cut pieces are stored in a silo where they **ferment** to become an energy-rich feed.

Weather, Diseases, and Pests

Corn is grown almost everywhere in the world, and crops must endure all types of weather conditions. The Corn Belt in the United States, where more than 80 percent of American corn is grown, overlaps Tornado Alley. Tornado Alley is an area that experiences many tornadoes throughout the spring and summer, and extends from southern Texas to southern South Dakota, covering parts of Kansas, Iowa, Nebraska and other states that are part of the Corn Belt. The winds of a tornado can reach 250 miles per hour (402 kilometers per hour) and destroy everything in its path, including corn crops. Severe tropical storms, as well as cyclones and hurricanes, which often hit Central America, the Caribbean, and the southern United States, can also ruin crops. Drought is another common problem in many parts of the world, including much of Africa and the American Corn Belt. Drought is a long period of time without enough rain. Soils remain dry and plants do not receive enough water to grow healthy.

(above) In 1986 and 1988, the Corn Belt went through a period of severe drought. Farmers produced less corn and many received money from the government to help them cover the cost of running their farms.

Pests

There are thousands of types of insects that feed on corn, many specific to certain regions of the world. Some insects can damage the entire plant while others prefer to eat specific parts, such as the kernels or leaves. The European corn borer is believed to have been introduced to the United States from Europe in the early 1900s. Today, the insect, which is a moth during its adult life, can be found throughout much of the United States and Canada. The moths lay eggs on the leaves of corn plants. The eggs then hatch into larvae, which feed on leaves and tunnel through corn stalks. The stalks often become so weak that they fall over, and ears of corn spoil, or rot.

▸ *European corn borers feed on more than 200 kinds of plants, including corn.*

Disease

Corn plants are affected by diseases that can damage parts of the plant or the entire plant. Corn smut, or common smut, is disease that is caused by a **fungus**. A corn plant infected by smut develops silvery-white galls, or growths, on the stalk, tassel, leaves, and ears. The galls that form on the ears are the largest, growing up to four inches (ten centimeters) in diameter. Eventually, the galls burst open and release thousands of tiny, black spores. Spores are the cells that fungi develop from. To prevent corn smut from ruining crops, galls must be removed from the plants before they rupture. This way, the spores, which are carried by the wind and infect other plants, do not get a chance to become air-borne.

(left) In Mexico, galls of corn smut are eaten, and considered a delicacy, or special food.

Feeding the World

Severe hunger and poverty are most common in developing countries, where people do not have the money to buy food. Cereal grains, including wheat, rice, and corn, are staple foods that prevent many people from starving. People who grow their own food often do not have the money to buy fertilizers or the chemicals that prevent insects, disease, and weeds from ruining their crops. Some of the most severe poverty in the world exists in **Sub-Saharan Africa**, where many areas are also prone to droughts, which leads to poor quality crops and low yields. People who live in poverty eat mostly staple foods that grow well in their area. Many people in Sub-Saharan Africa rely on corn to keep them alive.

(bottom) More than 14 million people face starvation in Africa. These women have received corn from an aid organization.

▾ Drought in developing countries devastates corn crops.

Dying for Food

Malnutrition is a condition in which people do not get enough of the vitamins and nutrients their bodies need to stay healthy. This can lead to many deadly diseases. People who suffer from malnutrition are physically weak and constantly feel tired. While corn and other grains can provide people with the energy they need to get through their day, a diet based almost solely on corn will lead to malnutrition. Corn alone does not have enough protein and vitamins to keep people healthy.

Millions of people around the world, many of them children, die from hunger or malnutrition each year.

Fighting Hunger

Many aid and peace organizations, such as the United Nations, are trying to fight hunger. Fighting hunger is more than simply providing food for hungry people. Farmers in developing countries need to be able to supply enough food for their families, and produce enough crops to sell as well. This will allow farmers to purchase supplies to grow healthier crops, such as fertilizers, irrigation equipment, pesticides, and high quality seeds. The International Maize and Wheat Improvement Center is an organization that develops corn seeds that will grow in harsh environments often common in developing countries. They have developed a type of corn called quality protein maize (QPM), which provides more protein than traditional varieties.

Glossary

breeding To cause a plant to produce seeds that will turn into new plants

cacao beans The seeds of the cacao tree, which are used to make chocolate

cell The smallest structure in any living thing

civilization A culture or society from a specific time and place

colonies Lands ruled by a distant country

commercial Intended for sale or profit

consistencies Texture of grain mixtures

cross-pollinate Using pollen from one plant to create seeds from another plant

cultivate To farm and harvest a crop

descendant A person who can trace his or her family roots to a certain family group

developing countries Poor countries that lack advanced technology

drought A long period without rain

empire A group of lands under a single ruler

ferment The process of sugars in food being changed into other substances

fungicide Something used to kill fungus

fungus A plant-like organism, including mushrooms and molds; some spread disease

gluten A protein that makes dough rise

Great Depression A period during the 1930s of high unemployment and a weak economy

greenhouse gas A gas in the atmosphere of the earth that makes the planet warmer

industrial Having to do with the making of goods for sale

irrigation system A way to move water to fields

New World The name Europeans gave to North, South, and Central America

plantation A large farm with many workers that usually specializes in growing one main crop

pollen A powdery substance plants make that helps to create seeds

protein A nutrient found in plants and animals

Sub-Saharan Africa Areas of Africa south of the Sahara Desert

tax Payments made to a government

tropical Hot and humid areas near the equator

West Indies A group of islands in the Atlantic

Index